Panorama-Books: PUERTO RICO

With thirty color plates

HANS W. HANNAU

PUERTO RICO

Argos inc.
PUBLISHERS
Miami and Munich

Wrapper and cover designed by Gerhard M. Hotop

Library of Congress Catalog Card No. 67–14183
Printed in Western Germany. 268
Wilhelm Andermann Verlag, Munich

*"One of the pleasantest things in the
world is going on a journey."*
WILLIAM HAZLITT

*Puerto Rico –
Success in the Making*

"Nothing," said Oscar Wilde, "succeeds like *excess!*" With respect to modern Puerto Rico, an excess of natural advantages, both natural and economic, does bring about success. Even if it has taken more than four hundred and fifty years.

For modern Puerto Rico is second to none of the Caribbean Islands in the profuseness of its marvelous scenery, historic interest, and cultural background, and in the inspiring economic development of recent years.

Puerto Rico's scenery runs the gamut from the pleasantly bucolic to the spectacularly mountainous, and the waters surrounding the island are the "bluest of Caribbean blue." Three hundred miles of coastline are fringed with smooth beaches of powdered sand, and only a few of the beaches have been developed.

Goethe said that no one feels at ease in a garden who does not like the open country. And this may be the secret of Puerto Rico's tranquility, for to be in Puerto Rico is to be at ease with one's surroundings. It is an island garden with the look of the open country, and nature has used a lavish palette of colors to paint a landscape of tropical loveliness.

History is everywhere in Puerto Rico, as one might expect in a land discovered in 1493 and inhabited continuously since that time. Evidence of Puerto Rico's historic importance is found mainly in the cities – San Juan, Ponce, Mayagüez, and others. The fortresses, churches, palaces, convents, cathedrals, and public buildings often date back two, three, and four centuries.

Puerto Rico today is a land of two cultures. The background of its people is Spanish, as are the language, music, dancing and food, befitting an island first settled in 1508 by Juan Ponce de León. Until the Spanish-American War of 1898, the island was a possession of Spain, although for a short period (1897) Puerto Rico enjoyed dominion status. Under the Treaty of Paris (1899), Puerto Rico passed from Spanish to United States sovereignty. For the past six decades, a patina of United States culture has been applied, arising from a free exchange of ideas with the new mother country. Witness, for example, the current interest in baseball, the supermarkets, condominium housing, luxury resorts.

In the field of economic development, Puerto Rico stands head and shoulders above its Caribbean neighbors. When it was occupied by the United States at the turn of the century, Puerto Rico was as impoverished as any other Caribbean Island. All the afflictions common to Latin-America and the Caribbean area were inherent there – lack of industry, an economy dependent on a single agricultural crop, great areas held by a few powerful landowners, and an enervating bureaucracy.

PUERTO RICO

Through Operation Bootstrap, the Puerto Rican government has boosted the per capita income until it is the highest in the Caribbean – and it still has a long way to go. Five hundred new industries have been established, ranging from small textile plants to the great Union Carbide plant at Ponce. Tourism is, of course, one of the major facets of Operation Bootstrap, and in this field alone Puerto Rico enjoys success that compares favorably with that of Jamaica and Nassau. A million and a half tourists leave more than $ 90,000,000 in Puerto Rico annually.

7

Virtually the whole population is dedicated to raising the standard of living, with an ever-increasing sense of social responsibility. Former Governor Luis Muñoz Marín, architect of Operation Bootstrap, once said, "We must live like angels and produce like devils." Today, Puerto Rico stands out like a beacon of progress in an extensive area of underdeveloped countries.

For the Puerto Ricans, however, economic development is only a means to an end. If they seek to improve their standard of living, it is because they have in mind the "good life," with the attendant blessings of education, health, housing, and cultural development. Hence *Operación Serenidad* – "Operation Serenity" – whose scope ranges from the restoration of old churches, houses, and forts to the rediscovery of folklore and old music.

"They change their climate,
not their disposition, who
run beyond the sea."
                    HORACE

Puerto Rico lies sixteen hundred miles southeast of New York in the Caribbean Sea. It is the last and most easterly of the great islands of the West Indies that curve out from the tip of Florida. From Puerto Rico, the smaller islands of the Lesser Antilles arch southward to the Spanish Main.

The island measures one hundred miles in length and forty miles in width and is the crest of an underwater mountain range. It emerges from the great Brownson Deep (27,000 feet) in the Caribbean, rising to its highest peak at Cerro de Punta, in the central part of the island, 4,398 feet above sea level. Here one will find cool mountain air and refreshing living quarters.

Puerto Rico lies within the tropics but is so far from the equator that the oppressive heat of the lower latitudes is unknown. Furthermore, there are no land barriers to the northeast within two thousand miles to break the force of the cool, prevalent trade winds, which bathe Puerto Rico the year 'round.

Within its rectangular shape, Puerto Rico contains all that is typical and beautiful in the Caribbean world – massive mountain ranges, wide, fertile plains, miles of shoreline, and beaches of shining sand bathed by a placid surf.

Nature has bestowed even more exotic gifts on the island, such as the Caribbean National Forest, on the slopes of Luquillo Mountain, which is filled with palms, giant ferns, bromeliads, and other colorful tropical flora. This is Puerto Rico's own "rain forest."

At La Parguera, on the southern shore, is Phosphorescent Bay, whose waters shimmer at night in a fairyland of flaming lights, caused by the world's largest concentration of bioluminescent plankton.

Pastel-colored reefs of pink and purple adorn the western and northern shores, which Columbus first sighted on his second trip to the New World in 1493.

> *"That far land we dream about,*
> *Where every man is his own architect!"*
> ROBERT BROWNING

"Its name is John!"

Columbus tarried just long enough in Puerto Rico to bestow its first name upon the island. According to tradition, the Great Discoverer said, "Joannes est nomen ejus" ("Its name is John"). Thus was John the Baptist christened by his father, old Zacharias, and these four Latin words are the official motto on the seal of Puerto Rico.

The island, which had been called Boriquén or Borinquén by the tribe of gentle Arawak Indians who greeted Columbus on his visit, was called San Juan Bautista for fifteen years after the discovery, until the arrival of that searcher of fountains of youth, Juan Ponce de León. Sailing into what is now the harbor of San Juan, he exclaimed, "*Que puerto rico!*" – "What a delightful [rather than 'rich'] port!" For reasons unaccounted for to this day, Puerto Rico became the name of the island and San Juan (The Baptist) was adopted as the name of the capital city.

Ponce de León became the first governor, establishing along with the first European settlers the Spanish cultural background of the island. Sugar cane was introduced in 1515 and became the island's main agricultural crop, remaining so for centuries. Tobacco came a hundred years later, and during the eighteenth century, coffee was introduced. Slavery was abolished in 1873.

For three centuries, the English, French, and Dutch fought with Spain for possession of Puerto Rico. Excepting the time when the English captured San Juan, holding it for a short time, the Spanish successfully fought off all comers, even the redoubtable Sir Francis Drake, who made a stab at seizing the island in 1595 after successfully sacking Santo Domingo. The guns of the mighty fortress of El Morro safely guarded the approaches to San Juan and Puerto Rico for the Spanish.

In 1897, Luis Muñoz Rivera, who is considered the George Washington or Simón Bolívar of Puerto Rico, won autonomy from Spain in the form of dominion status. But a year later United States troops landed in San Juan in the war against Spain, ending four hundred years of Spanish sovereignty.

With the cession of Puerto Rico to the United States five months later, the United States became a colonial power. In 1917, Puerto Ricans officially became American citizens, under the rule of the War Department. In 1952, the people of the island overwhelmingly approved a Constitution, which established the self-governing Commonwealth of Puerto Rico.

"The use of traveling is to regulate imagination by reality, and instead of thinking how things may be, to see them as they are."

SAMUEL JOHNSON

For most visitors to Puerto Rico, the gateway to the island is through the capital city and major port, San Juan. This is a wonderfully picturesque old Spanish city of narrow streets and great fortresses, built on one of the best-protected harbors in the world. It is also a modern, bustling metropolis, where hundreds of cars drive bumper to bumper.

The Old City was built on an island which today is linked to the mainland by bridges and causeways to form a peninsula not unlike that of San Francisco. The city long ago broke through its old protective walls to include the famous Condado section, the lively and beautiful *quartiers* of Santurce, Hato Rey,

11

and the university town of Rio Piedras. Santurce, alone, is larger than the original San Juan.

The city is figuratively bursting at the seams. Imposing resort hotels, the last word in splendor, are situated on suburban boulevards along the coast and in the vicinity of modern-as-tomorrow Isla Verde Airport. Each has its own garden setting, with beaches for backyards. There is water everywhere – sea, bay, two channels, and two lagoons.

From the Condado section, you drive into the city's main artery, Ponce de León Avenue, which is the heart of the shopping district. Here, chain stores and supermarkets from the United States vie in healthy competition with older, native-established shop from the Old City. Here, too, are neon-lighted movie theaters featuring English- and Spanish-language films. Night clubs and cabarets cater to an overflow business.

As you continue your San Juan – Condado – Santurce trip, possibly in one of San Juan's famous *guaguas* (buses), you will note the multi-storied, air-conditioned apartment buildings called "condominiums," where privately owned apartments sell for as much as $ 50,000 for four or five rooms. Middle-class private homes are going up in new developments beyond Santurce. These bear such names as Hyde Park, Eleanor Roosevelt, Truman, Beverly Hills, Santa Maria, Los Angeles, San Francisco.

The principal historical sights of San Juan are bunched conveniently for the tourist at the tip of the Old City, where an undiluted Spanish atmosphere prevails. These include El Morro Castle, the Fortaleza, Fortress San Cristóbal, the Cathedral, and the Church and Plaza of San José, among others.

Castillo de San Felipe del Morro, to give this fortress its proper name (Morro means a knoll or hillock), was the strongest bastion in the Western World and is the number-one sight in old San Juan. It sustained and repulsed attacks from the British, French, and Dutch for centuries. Two of those Irish-Spaniards whose names ring so colorfully through Latin-American history were responsible for bringing these fortifications to maximum strength – Alejandro O'Reilly and Tomás O'Daly.

When Admiral Drake attacked San Juan, attracted by the rumor that a great Mexican treasure fleet had arrived, a chance cannon shot from San Gerónimo struck the Admiral's dinner table, killing three captains who were dining with him. This so enraged Drake that he set fire to a Spanish ship in the harbor. The blaze illuminated his own fleet so brightly that the guns of El Morro were successful in destroying almost half of the Admiral's ships.

Covering more than 200 acres and rising 145 feet above the sea, El Morro was begun in 1539 and completed in 1586. Continual improvements were made, however, until 1787.

The fortress is now a national historic site. A guided tour of the ramparts and labyrinthine tunnels is highly recommended to all who are not allergic to climbing.

The Fortaleza (Fortress) is the official residence of the governor of Puerto Rico. This half-fortress, half-palace was begun about 1533, burned by the Dutch in 1625, and rebuilt in 1640 and 1845. It has been the residence of governors for more than three hundred years. The beauty oft its construction, setting, and seaside gardens is world-famous with antiquarians and is by far the most appealing official building in the entire Caribbean area.

The Cathedral of St. John the Baptist, just north of the Fortaleza, was begun in 1519 and rose again and again after successive burnings. The present edifice, a "liner laden with souls, holding to the east its hull of stone", dates back to 1892, with Gothic effects that go back to 1540. The remains of Juan Ponce de León are here, brought from the older church of San José.

The Church of San José is one of the oldest Christian places of worship still in use in the New World. It dates from 1523. Ponce de León was buried here for three and a half centuries until his remains were removed to the Cathedral. A statue of the first governor, forged from bronze cannon seized in 1797, stands outside in the Plaza. Next door to the church is the old Santo Domingo Convent, as fine an example of sixteenth-century Spanish colonial architecture as one is likely to find.

Ponce House or the Casa Blanca (White House) is the oldest habitable building in the New World. Situated near the ramparts of El Morro, the palace was built in 1523 as a residence for Ponce de León, who was then looking for the Fountain of Youth in Florida. His descendants inhabited the house for two hundred and fifty years and then sold it to the Spanish government. Today it is a national historic site.

A seventeenth-century convent for Carmelite nuns has been restored and renovated and turned into a charming hotel. Its name? El Convento.

Old buildings, old narrow streets cobbled with blue stones brought over as ballast in many a Spanish galleon, ruins of the Old City walls that formerly encircled San Juan, wrought-iron balconies, blue-tiled patios, all these combine to preserve an atmosphere of sixteenth- and seventeenth-century Spain-in-the-New World. It must be remembered that during colonial days San Juan was a fairly wealthy city, the residence of Spanish grandees and rich plantation owners whose homes, churches, buildings, and convents were among the most beautifully designed and decorated in the Caribbean. Despite modern introductions and intrusions, San Juan (the Old City) is still Spanish.

Before one leaves the city limits of San Juan for an excursion around the island, there are several other places one must see.

San Cristóbal Fortress was started a hundred years after El Morro and stands on the eastern tip of the Old City's shore line. This was to be the number-two defense point of San Juan, supplementing the mighty El Morro. These enormous defensive structures, very much like those in Havana and Santiago, Cuba, were considered impregnable in their day. A network of tunnels, closed today, under the city connects El Morro, San Cristóbal, and the Fortaleza with other strategic places in the city.

The Parque Muñoz Rivera is a spacious and idyllic pleasure park, named for the great patriot-statesman of Puerto Rico. The park overlooks the sea and faces San Juan's popular baseball stadium.

San Juan's new race track out in Rio Piedras is certainly worth a visit whether the horses are racing or not. It is called the Hipódromo de El Comandante and is a fine structure in a lovely setting.

The University of Puerto Rico, at Rio Piedras, is the pride of *portorriqueños*. Some of the newer buildings were constructed under the administration of Franklin D. Roosevelt, which spurred the university to new bursts of energy and ever-expanding activities. It has an enrollment of about twenty-five thousand students of both sexes and every shade of color from black to white. The university is "dedicated to the American Republics for the Advancement of Learning" and endeavors to reconcile the Spanish and Anglo-Saxon cultures in the Americas.

The visitor will certainly not want to miss the very modern Supreme Court Building or the stately Capitol, where the legislature meets, or the ruins of San Gerónimo Fortress – all of which he will see as he drives from Old San Juan to the Caribe Hilton, Condado Beach, La Concha, Sheraton, Da Vinci, and other luxury hotels in the Condado section.

With more than three thousand miles of very good roads, Puerto Rico makes it easy for the visitor to see the national and historical marvels outside the capital.

For a half day's trip out of San Juan, visit El Yunque (The Anvil), a forty-five-minute drive from the city. This is the superb tropical rain forest spoken of earlier – the Caribbean National Forest. El Yunque is actually the name of the mountain peak to which one ascends through a cool, exciting forest world with splashing mountain waterfalls. A restaurant and cabins are provided for those who wish to linger, ride horseback, or swim in the cold mountain pool.

On the return to San Juan, one may stop at Luquillo Beach, one of the most beautiful in the Caribbean. Fringed with palm trees, it is a sweeping half-moon of white sand, and gently slopes to the waterline. Picnics here are a favorite pastime.

For a visit to Ponce and the south coast, a minimum of two or three days should be allowed if one is to absorb all the wonders to be seen.

Ponce, Puerto Rico's second city, is called the "Pearl of the South." Not quite so cramped as San Juan's Old City, Ponce allowed itself room to build spacious Spanish patios, garden balconies, and colonial mansions. It is considered by many to be more colorfully Spanish than San Juan.

Ponce has two lovely *plazuelas,* with the Cathedral of Our Lady of Guadalupe between them. Probably the most-often photographed subject in the city is the old Ponce firehouse (now a museum), the Parque de Bombas. It is painted

16

View from Condado Beach Hotel
Vista desde el Hotel Condado Beach

Luquillo Beach
Playa de Luquillo

>

Castillo de San Felipe del Morro

Rio Piedras –
University of
Puerto Rico
Río Piedras –
Universidad de
Puerto Rico

Barranquitas, P. R.

Ancient Walls and Tower of La Fortaleza, South Facade, 16th century
La Fortaleza. Antiguas murallas y torre (fachada sur, siglo XVI)

The Fortaleza, Governor's Palace (Entrance)
La Fortaleza. Entrada del Palacio del Gobernador

Porta Coeli Church, San German
Iglesia de Porta Coeli. San Germán

The "Sweet Life" – Hotel Pool and Beach, San Juan
La "Dolce Vita" – Piscina y playa de hotel en San Juan

Sugar Cane Harvest near Aguadilla
Recogida de la caña de azúcar cerca de Aguadilla

Las Croabas (View from the Conquistador Hotel)
Las Croabas (vista desde el Hotel El Conquistador)

Cathedral in Ponce, P. R.
Catedral de Ponce, P. R.

School of Medicine, San Juan
Facultad de Medicina de San Juan

Icacos Island
Isla de Icacos

At El Comandante Race Track, P. R.
Hipódromo de El Comandante, P. R.

$>$

Patios in old San Juan
Patios de la antigua San Juan

Mountain Road in Puerto Rico
Carretera de montaña en Puerto Rico

Lagoon as seen from the Miramar Charterhouse Hotel in San Juan
Laguna vista desde el Hotel Miramar Charterhouse, en San Juan

*San Cristóbal's
Haunted Sentry Box
La Garita
de Los Duendes,
en San Cristóbal
<*

*Rain Forest at
El Yunque
El "bosque húmedo"
en El Yunque*

Beach at San Juan
Playa (San Juan)

The Famous Phosphorescent Bay at La Parguera
La Famosa Bahía Fosforescente de La Parguera

Country Transportation
Transportes en el campo

San Juan Gate –
Main Entrance from
the Sea to the
Historic Walled City
Puerta de San Juan.
Entrada principal,
desde el mar, de la
histórica ciudad
amurallada

Boca de Cangrejos. Punta Maldonado

Cathedral of San Juan Bautista
Catedral de San Juan Bautista

Walls of El Morro
Murallas de El Morro

in glaring red and black stripes and adorned with gray, yellow, and green ornaments.

Also in Ponce are the first Protestant church ever authorized in the Spanish dominions in America – a gift of Queen Victoria of England – and the new Ponce Intercontinental Hotel, a luxury hotel of spacious dimensions that has provided a powerful stimulus to the tourist trade in these parts. Here, too, is a monument to Puerto Rico's great musical composer, Juan Morel Campos. Among the latter's masterpieces are the "Juegos Florales," "The Symphony of Puerto Rico," and a number of exquisite piano pieces, often played by the island's leading pianist, Jesús María Sanroma.

Mayagüez is the third largest city of Puerto Rico and an important port. It lies at the western tip of the island. The embroidery and needlework for which the island is famous stem largely from Mayagüez enterprises. A branch of the University of Puerto Rico – the College of Agriculture and Mechanic Arts – is here, as well as an agricultural experiment station conducted by the United States government and reputed to house the largest collection of tropical plants in the New World.

The coastal route passes through the fishing village and resort of La Parguera, where that singular marvel of nature – "The Bay of Living Light," or Phosphorescent Bay – is situated. The waters cast off a luminous glow at night that it is almost possible to read by. Heading north, the motorist will visit San Germán, an extremely ancient town founded by Diego Columbus, the son of the Discoverer. The Porta Coeli Church here (1513) is a relic of great interest.

Rural Puerto Rico is, to some, the most charming part of the island. Here one sees the cabins of the *jíbaros,* as the peasants are called, tucked away behind trees and shrubbery throughout the countryside.

Although the mountains are not as awesomely majestic as those found in

Jamaica and Haiti, they are more easily accessible to the tourist. They are spectacularly scenic, particularly when one gazes down from the heights to the green plains below. For those who are especially fond of spending time in the coolness of mountain reaches, a visit to Barranquitas, site of one of Puerto Rico's luxury hotels, is called for.

Other sites, towns, villages, and islands to see are these: Arecibo, first settled in 1556, where an Indian cave with pre-Columbian drawings and carvings is to be seen; Aguadilla, founded in 1506, which claims to be the place where Columbus first set foot on Puerto Rican soil (although many other sites on the island dispute this, claiming the honor for themselves); Cabo Rojo, once the hideaway of the pirate Roberto Cofresi; Caparra, where the foundation of Ponce de León's first house, built in 1509, stands; Isla Caja de Muertos (Dead Man's Chest Island), which claims to be the spot that inspired the old sea chanty "Fifteen men on the dead man's chest, Yo-ho-ho and a bottle of rum"; Dorado Beach, twenty miles west of San Juan and the site of the magnificent resort constructed by Laurance Rockefeller; Vieques Island, an attractive and distinctive place where the inhabitants prefer to be called *viequenses* rather than *portorriqueños*. The eastern tip of Vieques is restricted to the United States Marines. St. Thomas in the Virgin Islands is clearly seen, although it is forty miles away.

"I hear America singing,
The varied carols I hear."
WALT WHITMAN

Culture addicts in general and music lovers in particular are familiar with the annual Casals Festival of Puerto Rico. A three-week series of concerts usually held in May and organized around the famous 'cellist Pablo Casals, it is a significant an event in the musical world as the Salzburg and Bayreuth music festivals. No other cultural occasion has placed Puerto Rico so squarely on the world's roster of important musical centers. The world's leading pianists, violinists, conductors, composers, and vocalists have appeared at the festival.

The popularity of the Casals Festival has spurred the development of other cultural pursuits on the island, with festivals of ballet, opera, Puerto Rican drama, and symphonic concerts.

"The body travels more easily than the mind."

JOHN ERSKINE

The resort world of Puerto Rico

Puerto Rico has experienced a veritable explosion of tourism in the past ten years, comparable to that of Barbados, Bermuda, Jamaica, Nassau, and the Virgin Islands. The ever-increasing number of tourists flocking to Puerto Rico all the year 'round has advanced beyond the dreams of the most optimistic tourist promotion board in the Caribbean. Newer and bigger hotels crop up every year to house the million and a half tourists who fly or sail to this "island paradise" annually.

Some of the hotels bear Caribbean-sounding names, from the oldest luxury resort the Condado Beach, Normandie and the Caribe Hilton to the newer ones – La Concha, El San Juan, Americana, El Convento, Sheraton, Sands, Howard Johnson's, Da Vinci, San Gerónimo Hilton, Hotel Racquet Club, Flamboyan, Pierre, Holiday Inn, Darlington, Diener Tower, Atlantic Beach, Dorado Beach, Miramar Charterhouse, Ponce Intercontinental, El Conquistador, Dorado-Hilton and Mayaguez Hilton.

The *bon vivant* too will find a host of gourmet delights, with strong Spanish accent, in the island's restaurants.

And when the sun goes down, Puerto Rico's night life really comes to life. Almost every entertainment star of the first magnitude has appeared in Puerto Rico.

Most of the luxury hotels offer tourists the excitement of government-sponsored gambling casinos and, consequently, an easier way to part with their money than merely to spend it on dining, dancing, and watching floor shows.

In Puerto Rico, the sportsman is king. Facilities and conditions for almost every kind of fishing are ideal. Renowned for the deep-sea fishing off its coasts, the island offers shallow-water and even lake fishing. Blue and white marlin, tuna, sailfish, dolphin, wahoo, mackerel, barracuda, bonito, kingfish, tarpon, snook, snapper, and bonefish are among the hundreds of species found in Puerto Rican waters.

Another aquatic sport is water skiing, and if one spends any time on the island one will certainly take up skin diving. Every big hotel has tennis courts, and a few hold international tournaments.

Golf enthusiasts will need no reminder of the superb courses at Dorado. Ramey Air Force Base has an eighteen-hole course, which is open to the public. There is a good nine-hole course in Ponce, and other new courses are being developed like one at Rio Grande, the new Berwind Country Club.

Most mountain resorts in Puerto Rico provide facilities for horseback riding. From the middle of December to the middle of February, the season for shooting water fowl is on.

Bowling, bridge, and chess clubs, fencing – a whole host of amusements – are available to those who seek them in Puerto Rico. And if one has come to Puerto Rico to enjoy relaxation, the island is perfect for that, too.

THE PLATES

View from Condado Beach Hotel

Here is the modern resort area of San Juan. To the right is La Concha Hotel, the emblem of which is shown in the giant shell (la concha, in Spanish) that crowns the beach front. Farther along are the equally palatial Puerto Rico Sheraton, Hotel Da Vinci, and other hostelries.

Luquillo Beach

Due east from San Juan is the magnificently popular public beach of Luquillo. It is ranked among the most beautiful beaches in the world: long, crescent shape fine white sands, a forest of coconu palms, waters always calm und clear.

Castillo de San Felipe del Morro

This great fortress is the chief tourist attraction of Old San Juan. Built by the Spanish at the northwest tip of the city from 1539 to 1586, it covers more than 200 acres and rises 145 feet above the Atlantic. The castle was continually improved until 1787. It is now a national historic site.

Rio Piedras – University of Puerto Rico

Pictured here is the attractive campus of the University of Puerto Rico, which was founded in 1903 and has now more than twenty-five thousand enrolled students. It has an agricultural experiment station, a school of industrial arts (the largest in the world), and many other faculties and facilities.

Barranquitas

This charming mountain town is almost in the center of the island. Because of its cool climate, it is a popular year-round resort and the center of the local tourist industry. It is the birthplace and burial site of a great statesman, Luis Muñoz Rivera, father of the recent governor of Puerto Rico. The gently sloping hills are characteristic of the ever-green countryside of the island's interior.

Ancient Walls and Tower of the Fortaleza, South Façade, Sixteenth Century

Also known as the Palacio de Santa Juan. Construction began circa 1533. Two Catalina, this was the first fort built to protect the harbor and the city of San sixteenth-century towers are among the earliest examples of military architecture in the Americas. It was seriously damaged during the Dutch attack in 1625. Reconstruction of the Fortaleza was done in 1640 and 1845.

The Fortaleza, Governor's Palace (Entrance)

The Fortaleza is one of the oldest executive mansions in continuous use in the New World. It has been the seat of civil government for centuries and the residence of most of Puerto Rico's governors. The nineteenth-century section has been recognized as one of the most beautiful buildings of the "Isabelline Style."

Porta Coeli Church, San Germán

This oldest church in the western hemisphere was built in 1513. The altar, wooden pillars, and heavy entrance doors are much the same as they were more than four centuries ago. The town of San Germán, in the southwestern part of the island, is one of Puerto Rico's most attractive locales and resembles a typical Spanish town of the time of the Renaissance.

Morro Castle

This interesting airview of the once strongest fortification in the Caribbean shows clearly its location on a promontory overlooking the main entrance to the important harbor. The tremendous walls of the fortress rise 145 feet above the sea. It was garrisoned by the U.S. Army 'til 1967.

The "Sweet Life" – Hotel Pool and Beach, San Juan

This picture, which epitomizes the resort attractions of San Juan, was taken at the Caribe Hilton. Tourism accounts for much of Puerto Rico's economic resurgence. Luxurious hotels abound mainly in and about San Juan – Caribe- and Gerónimo Hilton, El San Juan, Holiday Inn,

Americana, Da Vinci, Sheraton, Dorado Beach, La Concha, El Convento – and more in Ponce, Barranquitas, and La Parguera. Attracted by the warm sun, cool breezes, and Caribbean waters, tourists flock to enjoy la dolce vita Puerto Rican style.

Sugar cane Harvest near Aguadilla

Sugar cane is one of the agricultural staples of Puerto Rico's economy. In this picture, the sugar cane harvest is being reaped as it has been for hundreds of years. Aguadilla claims that it was close to here that Columbus first set foot on Puerto Rican soil.

Las Croabas (View from the Conquistador Hotel)

This is one of the more important fishing centers on the east coast of the island. Las Croabas is a quiet, peaceful place to relax, away from a tension-ridden civilization. Although becoming more and more popular with tourists, for whom a beautiful hotel, called the Conquistador, has been raised, Las Croabas retains its unspoiled look.

Cathedral in Ponce, P. R.

The city of Ponce is called the "Pearl of the South." One of its outstanding adornments is Our Lady of Guadalupe Cathedral, which dominates two lovely plazas.

School of Medicine, San Juan

The façade of the attractive School of Medicine in San Juan is typically Spanish in architecture. The surrounding gardens are ablaze with bougainvillaea, flame vine, oleander, and other tropical blooms.

Castillo de San Cristóbal – San Juan

Why was a new fortress in addition to El Morro needed to protect San Juan? The main purpose of this multi-level castle was to defend the city against land attacks. The temporary capture of El Morro by George Clifford, the Earl of Cumberland, demonstrated the great need for protecting the eastern approach to San Juan. This massive fortress, situated on the northeast corner of the city, was begun in 1634 on a promontory about half a mile from El Morro. In 1765, Charles III of Spain sent Field Marshal Alejandro O'Reilly to inspect the military structures of San Juan. The military engineer, Tomás O'Daly, incorporated French concepts of defense in depth. San Cristóbal, completed about 1783, was considered a defense system of the first order.

If El Morro Castle is a typical medieval example of defense by height, the massive fortress of San Cristóbal is an extraordinary illustration of the eighteenth-century military concept of defense in depth.

San Cristóbal Fortress is considered an exceptional example of the polygonal system of military architecture that was so in vogue in Europe when war was the hobby of monarchs.

In 1797, the English organized an expedition against this Caribbean Island under Sir Ralph Abercromby. It was unsuccessful. The United States Navy was the next to come. In 1898 San Cristóbal was the scene of an artillery duel between the harbor defenses of San Juan and Admiral Sampson's squadron. The Spanish-American War brought an end to the Spanish Empire in America and the beginning of a new era.

The fortification of San Juan had come a long way since Juan Bautista Antonelli made the first plans of El Morro in the sixteenth century and Tomás O'Daly designed the unequaled defenses in the eighteenth. To walk through the courtyard ramps of these historic bastions is to enjoy a visit to other centuries.

History and modern life in San Juan

Just over the palm trees in the center of the photo is seen the historic fort of San Gerónimo, one of the three small forts built to protect the landward end of San Juan Island. Finished about the end of the eighteenth century, it played an important role during the English attack of 1797. It is today a museum of consid-

erable importance in the culture of San Juan. Just beyond, we skip over a small body of water and almost two hundred years in time to modern San Juan's fabulous resorts. To the west is the San Gerónimo Hotel, to the right the Flamboyant Hotel, with La Concha and the Sheraton beyond them. The up-to-date city of San Juan is background to it all.

Icacos Island

Just outside Las Croabas is the delightful little island of Icacos. Lovely sandy beaches entice the mainlander to bathe in emerald-green waters. The island is popular, too, with boating enthusiasts.

At El Comandante Race Track

San Juan's modern race track provides an exciting experience in horse racing. It is one of Puerto Rico's major show places, with its beautiful infield of tropical shrubs and its beautiful lake, luxurious club house, and Spanish-American atmosphere.

Patios in Old San Juan

The pause that refreshes seems more so when taken in an old Spanish-style patio. Some of Old San Juan's ancient buildings have been converted into boutiques of distinction, with displays in the open air.

Mountain road in Puerto Rico

Puerto Rico has more well-graded highways and roads than any other Caribbean island. They lead along seashore and into the country for breathtaking views of the island's scenery.

Lagoon as seen from the Miramar Charterhouse Hotel in San Juan

Fashionable modern San Juan lies just over the waterway, where soaring luxury hotels of neon and marble vie with one another in modernity. Resplendent homes in rich residential areas abound, evidence of the growing importance and wealth of this loveliest of tropical Caribbean islands.

San Cristóbal's haunted sentry box

Legend says that the Devil spirited away soldiers manning this sentry point during the colonial wars. A more natural explanation is the underground passage that led directly from this point to a local wine tavern.

Rain Forest at El Yunque

This is a portion of the tropical rain forest that clothes the slopes of El Yunque, "The Anvil," in the northeastern corner of the island. It is a cool, magical world of giant ferns, exotic palms and other trees, wild orchids, bromeliads, brilliantly colored tropical flowers, and mountain waterfalls, all part of the Caribbean National Forest, where there is more than one hundred inches of rainfall per year.

Beach at San Juan

Fashionable tropical beaches such as this one are only minutes from wherever one may be staying. Palm trees sway in the breezes that emanate from the constant trade winds, and soft, pink sands fringe placid, crystal-clear waters to attract sun bathers and surf bathers alike.

The famous Phosphorescent Bay at La Parguera

At night these waters are luminous and opalescent, and when there is no moon the view is absolutely eerie. The phenomenon is caused by the peculiar plankton in the water, which even when bottled retains its luminosity for some time. In the daytime, the calm waters of La Parguera harbor are dotted with fishing boats and yachts. It is one of Puerto Rico's leading fishing ports.

Country Transportation

Side by side with modern vehicles of transportation are the centuries-old conveyances of cart and bullock that one sees everywhere along the countryside.

San Juan Gate – Main Entrance from the sea to the historic Walled City

This was once the main entrance to the walled city of San Juan and was completed in 1641. The view of the bay and the massive ramparts of the town are very impressive from here.

Boca de Cangrejos, Punta Maldonado

Completely unspoiled and almost wild-looking beaches such as this one at Punta Maldonado are favorites with those who appreciate nature off the beaten track.

Cathedral of San Juan Bautista

This is one of the oldest churches in the

western hemisphere. It is in Cristo Street, the oldest street in San Juan. The original palm-thatched structure dates from 1521 and was built by Alonso Manso, the first bishop of Puerto Rico. Damaged by a hurricane, the Cathedral was reconstructed in 1540. It is noted for its circular staircase and its ceiling in Gothic style. The Cathedral was enlarged and rebuilt in 1892. Ponce de León's remains have been moved from San José Church to a marble tomb in the Cathedral. The Cathedral museum contains a notable statue of a Madonna, sixteenth-century chalices, and many objects of historical and artistic value.

Walls of El Morro

Philip II of Spain, conscious of the need to fortify the Indies, commissioned General Juan de Tejeda to plan fortifications in all the important seaports of the Caribbean. Puerto Rico, being the most easterly of the islands and possessing a magnificent harbor, would become an excellent entrance to the Caribbean, the king thought, if well defended.

For the construction of the military defenses in Puerto Rico, the local royal funds, the voluntary services of the inhabitants, and funds from the treasury of Nueva España (Mexico) were used. The official design of the fortress, which came to be known as El Morro, was made by Juan Bautista Antonelli. Additions were later made by governors Pedro de Salazar, Menéndez, and Suares Coronel.

Like those in many other seaport towns of the Spanish Main, the fortress of El Morro was built on a promontory as an impregnable harbor defense. El Morro commanded the main entrance, assisted by a battery called Santa Elena, while El Morrillo and the Cabrón batteries took care of the eastern shore and the Boquerón Fort the shore end of the island of San Juan. In 1598, the artillery numbered eighty-eight pieces in all.

For an interesting description of the fort and the city of San Juan at the time of Cumberland's attack in 1598, we quote from the contemporary Reverend Layfield's narrative: "This Fort is to the seaward very strong and filled with goodly Ordnance and bestowed for the most advantage to annoy an ennemie that possibly could bee devised. The towne consisted of many large streets, the houses after Spanish manner, of two stories height onely but very strongly made and the roomes are goodly and large, with great doors instead of windows for receipt of aire. The Towne in circuit is not so bigge as Oxford but very much bigger than all Portesmouth within the fortifications and in sight much fayrer."

Acknowledgments

Julio Marrero Nuñez of the National Park Service in San Juan not only assisted me with valuable historical data but also guided me through the historic sites of San Juan while I was taking the pictures for this book. I very much appreciated his help, and I would like to thank also T. O'Conor Sloane III, editor, Doubleday & Company, Inc., for his editorial assistance.

HANS W. HANNAU

PANORAMA-BOOKS

USA: Arizona · California · California Missions · Cape Cod · Colorado · Florida Kentucky · Los Angeles · Michigan · New Jersey · New Orleans · New York · Palm Beach · San Francisco · Virginia · Washington D.C. · Yosemite

Caribbean: Aruba · Barbados · Curaçao · Guadeloupe · Jamaica · Martinique · Nassau Puerto Rico · Trinidad & Tobago · The Virgin Islands

Germany: Bavaria · Bavarian Alps · Bavarian Royal Castles · Berlin · The Black Forest · Bonn · Cologne · Essen · Hamburg · Heidelberg · Lake Constance Moselle · Munich · The Rhine · Romantic Germany · Romantic Main River · The Ruhr

Austria: Austria · Badgastein · Carinthia · Romantic Danube · Styria · Tyrol Vienna

France: Alsace · Brittany · Burgundy · Châteaux of the Loire · Corsica · Côte d'Azur · French Cathedrals · Mont Saint-Michel · Normandy · Paris · Paris by Night · Provence · Versailles

Italy: Capri · Florence · The Gulf of Naples · Pompeii · Rome · Sicily · Southern Tyrol · Venice

Scandinavia: Copenhagen · Denmark · Finland · Helsinki · Iceland · Lapland Norway · Sweden

Switzerland: Grisons · Lake Geneva · Lake Lucerne · Romantic Switzerland

Capitals of the world: Athens · Brasilia · Brussels · Istanbul · London · Moscow Peking · Rio de Janeiro · São Paulo

Other countries: Andalusia · Balearic Islands · Bermuda · Canada · Canary Islands Costa del Sol · Flanders · Greece · The Holy Land · Ireland · Israel · Japan Mexico · Morocco · New Zealand · Portugal · Rhodes · Scotland · South Africa Spain · Yugoslavia – Dalmatian Coast

Editor Hans Andermann